EAST COAS
PACIFIC
The Postwar Years

Peter Waller

UNIQUE BOOKS

Front cover: cOn 19 April 1954, 'A2' No 60527 Sun Chariot heads south from Aberdeen with a 10.5am special. Constructed at Doncaster (Works No 2018) and completed in January, No 60527 was the first of the class completed with initially an 'E' prefix to its original LNER number; it was physically renumbered by BR in June 1948. Delivered in LNER apple green, the locomotive, which was allocated to Dundee between June 1949 and April 1960, was repainted in BR green in May 1949.
John McCann/Online Transport Archive

Title page: Pictured awaiting departure from London King's Cross is No 60105 *Victor Wild*. When completed at Doncaster (Works No 1566) in March 1923, the locomotive was numbered 1474 in the GNR sequence; it became LNER No 4474 in 1924 and was the fifth of Gresley's original Pacific class to be completed. Named after the winner of the 1896 Kempton Park Jubilee Handicap, the locomotive was rebuilt as an 'A3' in October 1942. Renumbered 105 in May 1946, the locomotive was to be repainted in BR blue in March 1950 and into BR green almost exactly three years later. The locomotive was allocated to King's Cross from November 1942 through to September 1951 when it was transferred to Grantham. *D. Kelk/Online Transport Archive*

First published by Unique Books 2018
© Text: Peter Waller 2018
© Photographs: As credited

A CIP record for this book is available from the British Library

Unique Books is an imprint of Unique Publishing Services Ltd, 3 Merton Court, The Strand, Brighton Marina Village, Brighton BN2 5XY.
www.uniquepublishingservices.com

Printed in Poland

ISBN: 978 0 9957493 4 4

A note on the photographs
All of the illustrations in this book have been drawn from the collection of the Online Transport Archive, a UK-registered charity that was set up to accommodate collections put together by transport enthusiasts who wished to see their precious images secured for the long-term. Further information about the archive can be found at: www.onlinetransportarchive.org or email secretary@onlinetransportarchive.org

INTRODUCTION

Whilst three of the 'Big Four' at Nationalisation possessed Pacific type locomotives – the only exception was the Great Western – it was the LNER that bequeathed the largest number to BR. In all some 256 4-6-2s – both tender and tank – passed to the new ownership in January 1948 and, over the next two years a further 63 were to be completed to LNER designs as the final Class A2s and all of Peppercorn's 'A1' class were built at Darlington or Doncaster.

At the Grouping in 1923 the LNER inherited two classes of express Pacifics: the 'A1' class from the GNR and the 'A2' from the NER. The latter comprised two locomotives designed by Vincent Raven with an additional three being constructed during 1924; all five were withdrawn by 1937. Only two of Nigel Gresley's 'A1' design had also been delivered by the time that the GNR disappeared but a further 50 were constructed between February 1923 and December 1924. However, during trials against GWR 4-6-0 No 4079 *Pendennis Castle* in 1925, the GWR locomotive was shown to have superior performance which resulted in modifications to the design of the type with No 4480 (the future No 60111) being rebuilt as the first of the 'A3' class in July 1927. Between August 1928 and February 1935 a further 27 new Class A3s were delivered whilst the long process of converting the remaining 'A1s' to 'A3' commenced in February 1928. With the – controversial – conversion of the original Gresley Pacific – No 4470 *Great Northern* – into the first of Edward Thompson's planned 'A1' class in 1945, the surviving Gresley 'A1s' were redesignated Class A10. Only one 'A10' – No 68 (60068) *Sir Visto* – remained to be converted into 'A3' in January 1948 and this was completed in December that year. From the late 1950s onwards all were fitted with double chimneys and the majority were also to receive smoke deflectors in the early 1960s.

Gresley's other classic Pacific design was the 'A4'; the first of these superb streamlined locomotives emerged between September and December 1935. Nos 2509-12 all emerged in a striking silver livery with appropriate names to operate a high-speed service between King's Cross and Newcastle. The success of this service led to the construction of a further 31 examples between December 1936 and July 1938. Originally all were fitted with valancing over the motion; this was, however, removed during the war for ease of maintenance and never replaced. Four of the locomotives were fitted with Kylchap blast-pipes and double chimneys from new; the remaining members of the class were so treated in the late 1950s. One member of the class – No 4469 *Sir Ralph Wedgwood* – was destroyed by enemy action when York station took a direct hit during 1942 but the remaining 34 all passed to BR in January 1948.

Gresley's successor Edward Thompson sought to develop further classes of Pacific locomotive but his appointment during the war allied to his relatively short tenure as CME meant that the number of Pacifics that he designed was limited; he was, however, responsible for the much more successful Class B1 4-6-0. The first of Thompson Pacific classes to emerge was the 'A2/2'; this represented a rebuild of the six Gresley-designed 'P2' 2-8-2s that had originally been built for operation on the main line between Aberdeen and Edinburgh. There is some debate as to the rationale for the conversion, but all six were rebuilt between January 1943 and December 1944. These locomotives were destined to become BR Nos 60501-6. Whilst work was in hand converting the 'P2s', Thompson had also converted four 'V2' 206-2s then under construction into Pacifics. This work, completed at Darlington between May 1944 and January 1945, resulted in the 'A2/1' class (the future BR Nos 60507-10). The 'A2/3' was the result of authorisation received in April 1944 to construct 30 Pacifics capable of handling both passenger and freight traffic; these locomotives were constructed between May 1946 and September 1947 and were destined to become BR Nos 60500/11-24.

Thompson's other Pacific – designed to be the forerunner of a new 'A1' class capable of working express passenger services – was the rebuild of No 4470 *Great Northern*. This was completed in September 1945. The rebuilt locomotive incorporated an 'A4'-type boiler, lengthened wheelbase, double blast-pipe and chimney, and three cylinders with Walschaert valve gear. This locomotive was eventually to be designated Class A1/1.

Following Thompson's retirement in 1946, his successor – Arthur Peppercorn – oversaw the final development of the LNER Pacific family. The final 15 'A2' class locomotives – the future BR Nos 60525-39 – were built between December 1947 and August 1948 to a modified design. This included the shortening of the wheelbase by 2ft 7in, the incorporation of a self-cleaning smokebox and electric lighting. Peppercorn's other class of Pacific – the 'A1' – was similar to his version of the 'A2' but with larger – 6ft 8in – driving wheels. They were fitted with double blast-pipes and chimneys. The first of the class entered service in August 1948 and the last in December 1949.

In terms of livery, the LNER had largely adopted black during World War 2; however, with the return of peacetime conditions, the 'A4' class reverted to its garter blue livery whilst apple green was restored to the 'A3' and 'A10' classes. The early locomotives constructed by BR to the ex-LNER designs were also initially outshopped in apple green but gradually BR blue or green replaced the original LNER livery. The blue, however, was to be short-lived as Brunswick Green came to dominate and Classes A1 to A4 were ultimately all to operate in this livery.

Of the 4-6-2T classes, three were inherited from the NER and one from the Great Central. Numerically, the largest class was the 'A8'; these had originally been completed by the NER as 4-4-4Ts to a design by Vincent Raven and delivered between 1913 and 1922. Designed Class D by the NER and H1 by the LNER, the locomotives had a tendency to roll excessively at high speeds and so all were rebuilt, to a design by Gresley, between 1931 and 1936. The type had originally been planned to operate fast passenger services between Darlington and Newcastle and along the north-east coast. All remained in service until the end of 1956 but then withdrawal was swift, with all being taken out of service by the end of 1960.

The second largest of the ex-NER 4-6-2T designs – and the only one of the three originally planned to a Pacific – was the 'A7' class. Again designed by Raven, the class was conceived for use on heavy mineral trains and for shunting work. A total of 20 of the NER Class Y were built at Darlington Works between October 1910 and June the following year. Withdrawal of the class began in 1951 and all had succumbed by the end of 1957.

The third – and smallest – of the ex-NER 4-6-2T classes was the 10-strong 'Whitby Tank' class designed by William Worsdell to replace the earlier 0-4-4Ts in use on the steeply graded line between Whitby and Scarborough. Designated Class W by the NER, the locomotives were originally built as 4-6-0Ts at Gateshead between December 1907 and April 1908. However, operational experience indicated that the coal bunkers were insufficient and, as a result, all were rebuilt between 1914 and 1916 as 4-6-2Ts with enlarged bunkers. The first of the 'A5' class to be withdrawn was No 9790 during 1947 and two others – Nos 9792 and 9799 – were to be withdrawn by BR without being physically renumbered. The remaining seven were all taken out of service by the end of 1953.

The final class of 4-6-2T was the ex-Great Central Class A5. Designed by John Robinson, the GCR's Class 9N was produced for high-speed suburban services out of Marylebone to Aylesbury and High Wycombe. A total of 21 locomotives were built at Gorton Works between March 1911 and October 1917 with a further 10 being completed between January and June 1923 following the Grouping. One of these – LNER No 5447 – was withdrawn in 1942 but the remainder passed to BR. Gresley saw the design as worth perpetuating and a further 13 locomotives were built by Hawthorn Leslie between September 1925 and March 1926 for use around Middlesbrough. Gresley modified the original design with reduced chimneys and boiler fittings as the original locomotives had been built to the GC's more generous loading gauge. Under BR the ex-GCR locomotives were designated 'A5/1' and the modified Gresley design 'A5/2'. All remained in service at the end of 1956 but again all were withdrawn by the end of 1960.

Whilst none of the ex-LNER 4-6-2T designs survive in preservation, six examples of the 'A4' class do survive as do one of the 'A3' class – No 60103 Flying Scotsman – and one of the Peppercorn 'A2s' – No 60532 Blue Peter. Although no Peppercorn 'A1' was to survive from BR, the A1 Steam Locomotive Trust was successful in building the 50th example – No 60163 Tornado – which was the first main-line steam locomotive completed in Britain since 1960s when it was launched in 2008.

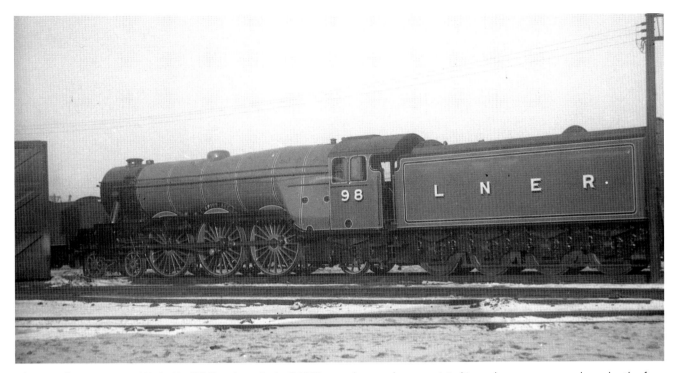

Above: Built at Doncaster (Works No 1710) and new in April 1929, No 98 *Spion Kop* was the last of the first batch of 10 Pacifics completed as 'A3s' from new. Originally numbered 2752, the locomotive was renumbered 561 in March 1946 renumbering – and, unlike most of those renumbered at the time, actually carried the March 1946 number – before becoming No 98 three months later and was repainted in apple green – as seen here shortly after work was completed – in March 1947. No 98 was to become BR No 60098 in November 1948 and was to retain its ex-LNER livery through until being repainted in BR blue in July 1950.
John McCann/Online Transport Archive

Right: Recorded shortly after the locomotive had been repainted into LNER blue in May 1947, 'A4' No 16 Silver King looks immaculate as it awaits its return to service. As No 2512, the locomotive was the third of the class to be completed, being built at Doncaster (Works No 1821) in November 1935. In the first 1946 renumbering scheme of 1946, the locomotive was allocated – but never carried – the number 582 but was to become No 16 in November of that year. It was renumbered BR No 60016 in April 1949 and was to be repainted from LNER blue to BR blue six months later. When the decision was taken to modify those members of the class that had not been constructed with a double chimney – four had been so fitted from new – No 60016 was the first to be modified in June 1957.
John McCann/Online Transport Archive

One of two Gresley-designed Pacifics to emerge prior to the Grouping of 1923, No 1470 was to become LNER 4470. Despite its historic significance (and for some it was an unfortunate choice), the locomotive was selected by Gresley's successor as the LNER's CME, Edward Thompson, to be rebuilt as part of his programme to construct two new Pacific classes – the 'A1' for express passenger traffic and the 'A2' for heavy passenger and freight duties. Plans for a number of new standard types had been developed since Thompson's appointment in 1941, but little progress was made until towards the end of World War 2. As rebuilt, the locomotive received Walschaerts valve gear, in place of Gresley's design, as well as new frames and an 'A4'-type boiler. The rebuilding work was completed at Doncaster Works in September 1945; the locomotive is seen here after its renumbering to 113 in October 1946. Thompson's original plans envisaged the conversion of others of Gresley's erstwhile 'A1' (now redesignated 'A10') type but No 113 was destined to be a one-off as Peppercorn's version of the 'A1' differed, with No 113 being designated Class A1/1. *John McCann/Online Transport Archive*

'A3' No 95 *Flamingo* stands in Carlisle station with a freight. The locomotive had been repainted in apple green in August 1947 and was to retain that livery through until reappearing in BR blue in December 1950. Built at Doncaster (Works No 1707) as LNER as No 2749, the locomotive was one of the first batch completed as 'A3s' from new. Renumbered 558 in March 1946 – one of a handful of the class to carry the early number allocated in the renumbering scheme – it was to become No 95 two months later. Physically renumbered by BR in September 1948, No 60095 had been allocated to Carlisle (Canal) shed for use on the Waverley route to Edinburgh for more than 30 years when withdrawn in April 1961. *Neil Davenport/Online Transport Archive*

Recorded at Doncaster with an Up service between May 1946, when the locomotive was renumbered, and November 1947, when the name *Kestrel* was replaced by that of *Miles Beevor*, No 26 had originally been built at Doncaster (Works No 1850) in February 1937 as No 4485. The locomotive was one of the few that carried, briefly (from April 1946), the first number – 587 – that it was allocated under the 1946 renumbering scheme. It is recorded here in the black livery that it wore between January 1942 and November 1947. It was to revert to LNER garter blue at that stage, being repainted BR blue in September 1949 and BR green in January 1953. Miles Beevor (1900-94) had worked with the LNER from 1943 and was the company's acting Chief General Manager at Nationalisation.
John McCann/Online Transport Archive

When completed at Doncaster (Works No 2024) in April 1948, No 60533 *Happy Knight* was the second of the 'A2' class to emerge bearing is BR number from new. Although painted in apple green on delivery, this was not to survive long as the locomotive, named after the winner of the 1946 2,000 Guineas, was repainted into BR green in December 1949 when it was also modified by being fitted with a double chimney. No 60533 was an English-based locomotive during its operational life, being allocated at various times to New England, Copley Hill, Grantham, King's Cross and Doncaster sheds prior to its withdrawal from New England in June 1963.

John McCann/Online Transport Archive

The third of the 'A3' class to be completed – at Doncaster (Works No 1695) in September 1928 – No 60091 *Captain Cuttle* was one of the class to receive an experimental – variously described as ultramarine or purple – livery in early BR days. Built as No 2745, the locomotive was named after the winner of the 1922 Derby (itself named after a character in the Dickens novel *Dombey and Son*). Notionally renumbered 554 in the first 1946 renumbering, the locomotive was to become No 91 in October 1946 and thus BR No 60091 when renumbered in April 1948 and when it was repainted into the purple livery – the first of the type to be so treated. The experimental livery was itself not to survive long and No 60091 re-emerged in BR blue in November 1949.
John McCann/Online Transport Archive

Although designed prior to Nationalisation, the first of the Peppercorn 'A1' class – No 60114 – was constructed at Doncaster (Works No 2031) and completed in early July 1948. For a week – from 11 July 1948 – it was displayed in an unnamed condition as part of a locomotive and rolling stock display at the works and is recorded here during that week. It was subsequently named *W. P. Allen* after a noted trade unionist and member of the Railway Executive. Originally outshopped in apple green but with 'British Railways' lettering, it was repainted BR blue in November 1949 and into green in August 1952. Spending most of its career on the Eastern Region section of the East Coast main line, withdrawal was eventually to come in late December 1964.
John McCann/Online Transport Archive

No 60021 *Wild Swan* is at Doncaster Works in mid-1948 for repair to accident damage. This was one of four members of the 'A4' class – the others being Nos 4, 22 and 27 – that operated briefly with the 'E' prefix to its number prior to renumbering; in No 60021's case, this was between February and September 1948 (when it was physically renumbered). No 60021 was new from Doncaster (Works No 1869) in February 1938 as No 4467. When recorded here the locomotive was in garter blue – having been repainted from black in April 1947 – and was to retain this livery until painted BR blue in March 1950. BR green was first applied in August 1951.
John McCann/Online Transport Archive

Pictured passing South Yorkshire Junction signalbox at Doncaster with the station in the background with the up 'Flying Scotsman' in October 1948 is Class A4 No 60023 *Golden Eagle*. Completed at Doncaster (Works No 1847) in December 1936 as No 4482, the locomotive had notionally been renumbered 584 in the initial 1946 renumbering scheme before becoming No 23 later in the year.

When recorded here, the locomotive was still sporting its LNER garter blue livery, having been renumbered in March earlier in 1948. No 60023 was repainted BR blue in August 1949 and BR green in September 1952. The new Doncaster South box, commissioned in January 1949, can be seen in the background. *John McCann/Online Transport Archive*

For a brief period – from 16 to 19 October 1948 – 'A4' No 60007 *Sir Nigel Gresley* was used to demonstrate the new Rugby test plant, which was officially opened in October that year. No 60007 was one of three 'A4s' – the others being Nos 60023 and 60034 – to emerge with their BR numbers, the first of the class to be so treated, when they were outshopped in March 1948. At this date the locomotive was still painted in the LNER garter blue livery; this had been reapplied in March 1947. As with other members of the class, the locomotive was repainted in BR lined out blue. This livery was to last from September 1950 through to April 1952 when No 60007 emerged in lined out green. As No 4498, the locomotive had originally been completed at Doncaster (Works No 1863) in November 1937. No 60007 was to survive in service until February 1966 and was to be preserved on withdrawal. *John McCann/Online Transport Archive*

Class A3 No 60102 *Sir Frederick Banbury* was the second of Sir Nigel Gresley Pacifics to be completed. Built by Doncaster (Works No 1539), the locomotive – as GNR No 1471 – entered service in July 1922. Sir Frederick Banbury was a politician and businessman. His role as the final chairman of the GNR was recognised in September 1922 when No 1471 was named after him. It became LNER No 4471 the following year and was to be rebuilt as an 'A3' in October 1942; it was to survive through until withdrawal in November 1961. It is seen here, whilst based at Leicester shed, at Leicester Central station ready to take over the Up 'The Master Cutler' during the late summer of 1949.
John McCann/Online Transport Archive

Pictured in apple green an unnamed No 60120 stands at King's Cross awaiting departure with the Down 'Yorkshire Pullman' in 1949. The locomotive was completed at Doncaster (Works No 2037) in December 1948 and was allocated to King's Cross shed from new. It was to retain its apple green livery until it returned to service, following overhaul, in March 1950 when it reappeared in blue. Named at the same time *Kittiwake* – one of only six of the class named after birds – No 60120 was transferred to Copley Hill shed in June 1950. It was to be based there for more than a decade prior to a final transfer – to York – in September 1963. *Neil Davenport/Online Transport Archive*

It is 1949 and a brand-new and unnamed Class A1 No 60146 is the centre of attention. The locomotive was completed at Darlington (Works No 2065) in April 1949 and would be eventually named *Peregrine* in December 1950 (a name previously carried by the 'A4' Pacific No 60034 *Lord Farringdon*). The photograph shows to good effect the plain topped chimneys that the locomotives were initially fitted with. When new, No 60146 was completed in LNER apple green livery with the legend 'BRITISH RAILWAYS' on its tender. It was to be repainted in BR blue contemporaneously with its naming but was to retain this livery for only a year, emerging in BR green in December 1951 following overhaul at Doncaster. No 60146 was to survive in service until October 1965, being sold for scrap the following month.

John McCann/Online Transport Archive

This and the next two views taken at Whitby in August 1949 show the railway in transition. The first of the trio portrays 'A8' No 9890 still retaining in LNER number and livery. This was one of the 45-strong class originally built as 4-4-4Ts and converted to 4-6-2T between 1931 and 1936. No 9890 was to become the penultimate of the class to retain its LNER identity, not being physically renumbered until June 1950; conversely, it was one of the first to be withdrawn, succumbing in January 1958.
Neil Davenport/Online Transport Archive

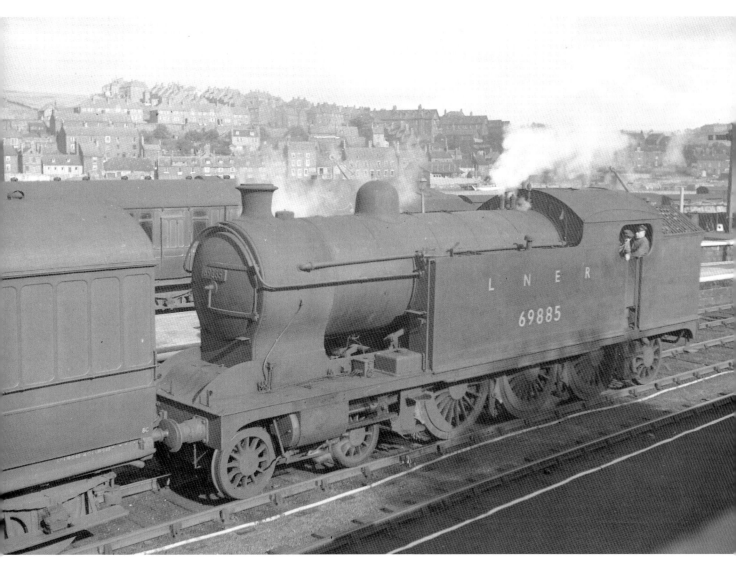

Although 'A8' No 69885 had been renumbered physically – during August 1948 – the locomotive still retains the 'LNER' title on its side tanks. Like all of the class, No 69885 was constructed at Darlington Works; it was completed there as North Eastern Railway No 1526 in September 1921, a number that it retained through until the 1946 renumbering scheme when it became No 9885. *Neil Davenport/Online Transport Archive*

Pictured on shed sporting its BR number – as physically renumbered in December 1948 – and with 'BRITISH RAILWAYS' on its side tanks, is one of the 'A6' class. In 1907 William Worsdell introduced a 10-strong class of 4-6-0T to handle services over the steeply-graded line between Whitby and Scarborough. Built at Gateshead Works, the class was designed to replace older 0-4-4Ts and became known as 'Whitby Tanks'. However, they lacked coal capacity and all were rebuilt between 1914 and 1916 by Vincent Raven to 4-6-2T. Nine passed to BR in 1948, but they were destined to have a short life in BR ownership; all had been withdrawn by the end of 1953, No 69794 having succumbed in August 1951.

Neil Davenport/Online Transport Archive

Recorded at its home shed, Grantham, on 7 May 1950 is 'A2' No 60133 *Pommern*. The locomotive had only been outshopped from Doncaster Works following a general repair the previous month in BR blue; it was named after the winner of the 1915 2,000 Guineas at the same time. No 60133 was completed at Darlington (Works No 2052) in October 1948 and initially emerged in LNER apple green livery. It was to retain BR blue until June 1952.
Peter N. Williams/Online Transport Archive

Also seen on Grantham shed that day was 'A4' Pacific No 60014 *Silver Link*. Completed at Doncaster (Works No 1818) in September 1935 and originally No 2509, No 60014 was the first of Nigel Gresley's classic 'A4' type to be completed. Becoming No 14 as a result of the LNER's 1946 renumbering scheme – having originally been allocated the number 580 earlier in the year – No 60014 was one of the first of the class to be repainted in BR blue – in June 1949 – and was allocated to Grantham between June 1948 and May 1950; it was transferred to King's Cross shortly after the date of this photograph and was to emerge in BR green in January 1952.
Peter N. Williams/Online Transport Archive

Organised by George Lake, the Great Northern Railway 'Centenary Express' operated on 16 July 1950 and ran from King's Cross to York via Spalding, Boston and Lincoln on the outbound journey and return behind, appropriately, No 60113 *Great Northern*. Scheduled to depart from London at 8.55am, it arrived three minutes early – at 2.4pm – in York, where it is recorded here with its train of six Pullman coaches and two kitchen cars. The headboard featured the face of Sir Edward Beckett-Denison (1787–1874), who was one of the leading promoters of the GNR and chairman of the company between 1847 and 1864. On the return journey, No 60113 ran through a set of level crossing gates at Selby. Whilst the train was stopped, some of the passengers retrieved sections of the splintered gates, which the train's driver autographed during a booked stop at Peterborough. Withdrawn in November 1962 with a badly worn cylinder, No 60113 was scrapped despite some efforts being made to see it preserved. *Peter N. Williams/Online Transport Archive*

Completed by North British in November 1924 as LNER No 2581 (Works No 23119), No 60082 *Neil Gow* – named after a race horse that had won the 1910 2,000 Guineas at Newmarket – was rebuilt as an 'A3' in January 1943. Allocated to Heaton shed at Nationalisation, it is seen here light engine at Glasgow Queen Street, not far from where it was built, on 25 March 1951. No 60082 was to withdrawn from another Tyneside shed – Gateshead – in September 1963.
Tony Wickens/Online Transport Archive

Heading the Up 'Scarborough Flyer' at Retford, south of the flat crossing, is the second of Peppercorn's 'A2' class to be completed, No 60526 *Sugar Palm*. Although completed at Doncaster (Works No 2017) in January 1948, the locomotive emerged as LNER No 526 in apple green livery; The next five locomotives all emerged with an 'E' prefix before their running number whilst from No 60532 the class appeared with their BR number from new. No 526 was physically renumbered in August 1948 and was repainted in BR green in October 1949. Based on the North Eastern Region – at either York or Neville Hill – for its entire career, No 60526 was withdrawn in November 1962, one of the first of the class to be taken out of service.

John McCann/Online Transport Archive

Class A4 No 60006 *Sir Ralph Wedgwood* is seen one mile north of Retford with the Up 'Capitals Limited'. This locomotive, completed at Doncaster (Works No 1868) in January 1938, had originally been LNER No 4466 when new and, until January 1944 (when it was renamed after the LNER's chief officer from 1923 to 1939 and the chairman of the wartime Railway Executive Committee from 1939 until 1941) it bore the name *Herring Gull*. There had been an earlier locomotive named after Sir Ralph Wedgwood – No 4469 – but this had been destroyed at York in June 1942 following a German raid. When recorded here, No 60006 was in BR blue, having been repainted in May 1950. It was not to retain this livery for long as it was to re-emerge in BR green in October 1951. *John McCann/Online Transport Archive*

Pictured heading southbound past Retford North signalbox is Class A1 No 60140 *Balmoral*. Completed at Darlington Works in December 1948, No 60140 was only a few years old when recorded in this view. The locomotive, as with the remainder of the class, was fitted with a plain topped chimney – clearly visible in this view – but these were subsequently to be replaced with lipped-top chimneys. Retford North box controlled the main line approaches to Retford station as well as the connection heading west towards the ex-Great Central line from Sheffield to Lincoln; the former GNR box was to survive until closure on 24 April 1976. *John McCann/Online Transport Archive*

Approaching Edinburgh Waverley from the west, having just emerged from The Mound Tunnel, in July 1950 is Thompson Class A2/1 No 60509 *Waverley*. This locomotive was completed at Darlington (Works No 1944) as LNER No 3698 in November 1944. Notionally allocated the number 886 in the first 1946 renumbering, the locomotive became No 509 in May 1946. The four members of the 'A2/1' class were originally scheduled to be constructed as 'V2' class 2-6-2s but Thompson gained authorisation in August 1943 that the four be built as Pacifics similar to the six that were to be converted from the 'P2' class 2-8-2s. Not wholly successful as a design – they were under-boilered and lacked adhesion – all four were withdrawn between August 1960 and February 1961.
Neil Davenport/Online Transport Archive

Also recorded at Waverley station – albeit at the east end – in July 1950 is 'A3' class No 60065 *Knight of Thistle*. This had originally been built as an 'A1', LNER No 2564, at North British (Works No 23102) in June 1928 and was only converted into an 'A3' in March 1947 – only eight of the class remained to be so treated at the start of that year and all bar two of these were released to traffic by the end of 1947. Notionally renumbered 533 in early 1946, it became No 65 in October 1946 and was physically renumbered by BR in July 1948. When recorded here the locomotive was in BR blue livery – having been repainted in November 1949 – and it was to retain this livery until reappearing in BR green during December 1952.
Neil Davenport/Online Transport Archive

Completed at Doncaster (Works No 2019), Peppercorn 'A2' No 60528 *Tudor Minstrel* was to enter service as No E528 in February 1948. Physically renumbered in June 1948, the locomotive was to be repainted from LNER apple green into BR green during June 1949 and it is in this condition that the locomotive is seen departing from Aberdeen. The locomotive was named after the winner of the 1947 2,000 Guineas. Allocated to Gateshead when new, the locomotive was transferred to Dundee in June 1949 and was to remain a Scottish Region locomotive for the remainder of its career, being withdrawn from Aberdeen shed in June 1966. *John McCann/Online Transport Archive*

Heading south from Aberdeen is No 60537 *Bachelor's Button* with a short freight service. Built at Doncaster and completed in June 1948 – one of two delivered that month – No 60537, like all the class except No 60525, was named after a racehorse. Originally allocated to Leeds Copley Hill, No 60537 was to spend the bulk of its career in Scotland; it was to be withdrawn from St Margarets shed in Edinburgh at the end of December 1962 and was cut up 18 months later at a scrapyard in Airdrie.
John McCann/Online Transport Archive

Seen on 6 April 1952 in ex-works condition at Doncaster, albeit without its tender, and newly painted into BR green is 'A1' No 60138 *Boswell*. The locomotive was one of those constructed at Darlington (Works No 2057) and was completed, in apple green livery, in December 1948. Allocated to York when new, the locomotive was to remain allocated to that shed for its entire operational life. It was to wear apple green for a relatively short period, being repainted BR blue in September 1949 and was named exactly a year later after the winner of the 1936 St Leger. Surviving in service for almost 17 years, No 60138 was to be withdrawn in October 1965.
Tony Wickens/Online Transport Archive

John Robinson designed a single class of 4-6-2T for the GCR; this was to become the LNER Class A5. The type was planned for express passenger workings on the suburban services from Marylebone to Aylesbury and High Wycombe. The first 20 were built prior to the Grouping in 1923 at Gorton Works; a further 10 emerged during 1923 whilst an additional 13 were constructed to a slightly modified design between September 1925 and March 1926.

The original GCR design was designated eventually Class A5/1 whilst those built to Gresley's modified version became Class A5/2. One of the original 'A5/1s' – No 69814 (built at Gorton in December 1912) – is pictured just outside Marylebone station on 14 April 1952. As the new 'L1' class 2-6-4Ts were introduced to the Marylebone services, so a number of the 'A5/1s' were transferred to north Lincolnshire. *Julian Thompson/Online Transport Archive*

With the station buildings of Rugby Central visible on the A428 road bridge in the background, 'A3' No 60059 *Tracery* heads a southbound service over the Great Central main line. Completed at Doncaster (Works No 1614) in March 1925 as LNER No 2558 the locomotive was named after an American-bred but British based racehorse that achieved fame through winning the 1912 St Leger.

Renumbered 90 under the LNER renumbering scheme, the locomotive was rebuilt from an 'A1' in July 1942. Based at King's Cross shed at Nationalisation, the locomotive was subsequently allocated to Leicester Central before a final return to 'Top Shed' in April 1957, from where it was withdrawn in December 1962.
John McCann/Online Transport Archive

Viewed looking southwards, Class A3 No 60090 *Grand Parade* stands at Rugby Central with a Down service towards Leicester and Nottingham. Note the wonderfully basic station indicators on the extreme left of the photograph. No 60090 was built at Doncaster (Works No 1694), being completed in August 1928 and was originally LNER No 2744, becoming No 90 under the LNER's post-war renumbering scheme. As completed, No 2744 was the second Pacific to be built as an 'A3' from new and was named after the winner of the 1916 Derby. No 60090 was to remain in service until October 1963.
John McCann/Online Transport Archive

Approaching Rugby Central from the north with the Up 'South Yorkshireman' is Class A3 No 60054 *Prince of Wales*. Completed at Doncaster (Works No 1609) as 'A1' No 2553, the locomotive was originally named *Manna*; it was renamed in December 1926. Rebuilt as an 'A3' in July 1943, the locomotive was renumbered 522 in March 1946; it carried this number through until September 1946 when it became No 54. Physically renumbered in April 1948, the locomotive – allocated to Leicester between February 1949 and June 1956 – bore BR blue livery from April 1950 through to November 1951 when it was repainted into BR green.
John McCann/Online Transport Archive

Recorded heading southbound from Aberdeen is the first of the Arthur Peppercorn-designed Class A2 Pacifics, No 60525 *A. H. Peppercorn*. Following the retirement of his predecessor, Edward Thompson, Peppercorn redesigned the 'A2' class. The modified design had a shorter wheelbase – by 2ft 7in – and slightly relocated cylinders along with a self-cleaning smokebox. In all, 15 of the modified design were completed but only one – No 525 in December 1947 from Doncaster Works – prior to Nationalisation. *John McCann/Online Transport Archive*

No 60525 is pictured again, this time heading south from Aberdeen with an Up service. When new the locomotive was painted LNER apple green – as were a number of other early examples of the class – but this livery was to be short-lived as repainting of the locomotives in BR Brunswick Green began in 1949. No 60525 was to survive in service until March 1963. *John McCann/Online Transport Archive*

During the summer of 1952 Class A1 No 60131 – by now fitted with a lipped top chimney – heads an Up service through Potters Bar station past the box at the north end of the station. North of the station the East Coast main line was quadruple but only double track south through the station southwards until the line was quadrupled. No 60131 *Osprey* was one of the earliest members of the class to be constructed, being completed at Darlington (Works No 2050) in October 1948. Originally unnamed, it was named in June 1950 the name *Osprey* having been previously carried by an 'A4' – No 4494 (BR 60003) *Andrew K. McCosh* – and was to be repainted from BR blue to green in September 1951 at about the time it was reallocated from King's Cross to Grantham shed. In its later life, No 60131 was one of the class allocated to Leeds Neville Hill, where its duties included work over the Settle & Carlisle and Waverley routes with services from Leeds to Edinburgh. It was withdrawn from Neville Hill in October 1965 and sold for scrap the following month.
John McCann/Online Transport Archive

Again, it's the summer of 1952 and 'A1' No 60157 *Great Eastern* heads from London King's Cross at Potters Bar. Completed at Doncaster (Works No 2051) in November 1949, No 60157 was the fifth of the class to be delivered in BR blue livery from. When recorded here, however, the locomotive had been repainted into BR green – a transformation that occurred in November 1951 when the locomotive was named after one of the constituent companies of the LNER. Allocated to King's Cross when new, No 60157 was based at Grantham when recorded here. It was to return to King's Cross in September 1956 before a final transfer to Doncaster in September 1958 from where it was withdrawn in December 1964.

John McCann/Online Transport Archive

On 28 September 1952 'A4' No 60007 *Sir Nigel Gresley* was employed to haul the 'Centenaries Express' from King's Cross to York and return. The train, which was privately promoted by a number of individuals (including Alan Pegler, the future owner of No 60103 *Flying Scotsman*), was organised to mark the centenary of the opening of the route from Peterborough to Retford via Grantham and Newark along with King's Cross station itself. The northbound trip was made via the East Coast main line but the return journey was run via Retford, Lincoln, Boston and Spalding. Here No 60007 is pictured light engine at York prior to its return to London at 3.5pm.

John McCann/Online Transport Archive

In the autumn of 1952, 'A3' No 60108 *Royal Lancer* heads south from Rugby Central station with the Up 'Master Cutler'. Built as LNER No 4477 at Doncaster (Works No 1569) and completed in May 1923, the locomotive was rebuilt as an 'A3' in October 1946. It had been renumbered 507 in March 1946 – and bore the number briefly – before becoming No 108 two months later. When recorded here the locomotive had just been allocated to Neasden; it was to be transferred to King's Cross in March 1953. At this date the locomotive was still in BR blue; it was to be repainted BR green in November 1952.
John McCann/Online Transport Archive

Pictured departing from the east of Edinburgh Waverley station is Class A3 No 60090 *Grand Parade*. The original locomotive had been built at Doncaster (Works No 1694) as LNER No 2744 and entered service in August 1928. The locomotive was named after the Irish-trained horse Grand Parade, which won The Derby in 1919 – the first black horse to do so for 106 years. On 10 December 1937 No 2744 was seriously damaged in an accident at Castlecary in Scotland; although notionally 'rebuilt', the No 2744 that emerged from Doncaster Works was effectively a new locomotive constructed from spare parts. (The LNER, like a number of other transport operations, built 'new' locomotives on the revenue, rather than the capital, account.) The new locomotive became No 90 during the LNER's renumbering scheme and thus No 60090 at Nationalisation. It was to be withdrawn for scrap from St Rollox shed, in Glasgow, at the end of October 1963.
John McCann/Online Transport Archive

Class A4 No 60009 *Union of South Africa* awaits departure from Edinburgh Waverley with a northbound service towards Dundee and Aberdeen. Completed at Doncaster (Works No 1853) in June 1937 as LNER No 4488, the locomotive was initially scheduled to be named *Osprey* but this was changed to *Union of South Africa*. Renumbered 9 under the LNER's post-war scheme and thus 60009 at Nationalisation, the locomotive carried BR blue from 1949 through to repainting in green in October 1952. It is seen here in the latter livery, in which it operated through to withdrawal in early June 1966. Preserved on withdrawal by John Cameron, No 60009 spent some time based on the Lochty private railway in Fife before being returned to the main line in 1973. A familiar sight on steam specials, particularly in Scotland, No 60009 was used to haul the official reopening train on 15 September 2015 that marked the restoration of services over the northern section of the Waverley route.
John McCann/Online Transport Archive

Whilst most are familiar with the striking lines of the Forth railway bridge, few have had the privilege of travelling across the bridge on the footplate of an 'A4' Pacific. Having recorded No 60009 at Edinburgh Waverley, the photographer then travelled north with the crew and took a number of striking images of the bridge from the engine. Some 40 years after the date of this photograph, No 60009 was again to make the journey across the Forth; in May 1994 it was transported by road from its depot at Markinch to travel to Bridgnorth for repair. It can thus claim the unique feat of being the only locomotive to have crossed the Forth by both the rail and original road bridge.

John McCann/Online Transport Archive

Pictured at its home shed – Aberdeen to where it had been transferred from Gateshead in August 1949 – is Peppercorn 'A2' *Bahram*. When delivered from Doncaster (Works No 2022) in March 1948, the locomotive had been numbered E531 – the last of five members of the class to be completed with the 'E' prefix – and painted in apple green. The locomotive was named after the winner of the 1935 Triple Crown in 1935, by winning the 2,000 Guineas, the Derby and the St Leger in the one year. One of the first of the class to be repainted in BR green – in June 1949 – No 60531 was to remain a Scottish Region locomotive for the bulk of its career, a final transfer – to York – taking place in December 1962 shortly before withdrawal.

John McCann/Online Transport Archive

Between 1913 and 1921 the North Eastern Railway constructed 45 4-4-4Ts to the design of Sir Vincent Raven – he was knighted in 1917 – at Darlington Works. These all passed to the LNER in 1923 and became the 'H1' class. Following experience with the 'A5' class and the conversion of one of the class – No 2162 – into a 4-6-2T, a series of trials was undertaken. This showed that the Pacific design offered greater stability at speed with the result that the remainder of the class were rebuilt as Pacifics between 1933 and 1936. As rebuilt, the locomotives were used on heavy suburban and coastal routes, being allocated to a number of ex-NER sheds, including Neville Hill in Leeds and Whitby. On 26 July 1953 No 69851 is seen near Darlington North Road. This locomotive, built originally as NER No 2144 (a number it retained at Grouping) at Darlington Works in October 1913, was rebuilt in March 1935. No 69851 was to be withdrawn from West Auckland shed in November 1958. *Tony Wickens/Online Transport Archive*

Operating between 1947 and 1966, the 'Norseman' was a service that operated between King's Cross and Newcastle Tyne Commission Quay, where it connected into ferry services operated by either Bergen Line or Fred Olsen across the North Sea to Norway. See here with the Up service is Peppercorn 'A1' No 60148 *Aboyeur*. This locomotive was completed at Darlington (Works No 2067) in May 1949 and emerged in the BR version of apple green with 'BRITISH RAILWAYS' on the tender. Named in January 1951 – after the winner of the 1913 Derby – the locomotive was repainted in BR blue at the same time. It retained this livery until July 1952 when it re-emerged in BR green with the early logo and it is in this condition when recorded here. Allocated to the Eastern Region for its operational life – at Ardsley, Copley Hill, Grantham and King's Cross sheds – No 60148 was withdrawn in June 1965. *John McCann/Online Transport Archive*

The Down 'Yorkshire Pullman' is seen behind Class A4 Pacific No 60025 *Falcon* working hard on the approaches to Finsbury Park. As LNER No 4484, the locomotive was completed at Doncaster Works (Works No 1849) in January 1937 and at Nationalisation was allocated to King's Cross shed. No 60025 was withdrawn from New England shed, Peterborough in late October 1963. The 'Yorkshire Pullman', known by that name from 30 September, 1935, had previously run as the 'Harrogate Pullman Limited' from its launch in 1923 and as the 'West Riding Pullman' from renaming in 1928. By 1950, the popularity of the service resulted in it being formed of 11 carriages, providing accommodation for 108 first- and 192 third-class passengers.

John McCann/Online Transport Archive

The only 'A2' to survive in preservation – No 60532 *Blue Peter* – heads a short freight southbound from Aberdeen. Completed at Doncaster (Works No 2023) in March 1948, No 60532 was the first of the class to appear bearing its BR number from new. Delivered in LNER apple green, the locomotive – which was named after the winner of the 1939 Derby and 2,000 Guineas – was repainted in BR green during September 1949; the locomotive was fitted with a double chimney at the same time. Although initially allocated to York when new, No 60532 was to spend the bulk of its career in Scotland, being allocated to Aberdeen, Dundee and Haymarket sheds. Withdrawn at the end of December 1966 – the last of the class to survive – No 60532 was rescued for preservation, backed by the viewers of the popular BBC children's television programme of the same name, in March 1968.
John McCann/Online Transport Archive

Pictured awaiting its next duty at Heaton shed – its home shed – on 10 October 1954 is 'A3' No 60077 *The White Knight*. This was one of the class completed by the Glasgow-based North British Locomotive Co (Works No 23114) and entered service in October 1924. Originally numbered 2576 by the LNER, the locomotive was rebuilt as an 'A3' in July 1943. Latterly based at St Margarets shed in Edinburgh, No 60077 was to survive until July 1964.
Tony Wickens/Online Transport Archive

Class A3 No 60049 *Galtee More* emerges from the southern portal of Catesby Tunnel, to the north of Charwelton station, with the Up 'Master Cutler' during the late spring of 1955. Completed at Doncaster (Works No 1604) in September 1924, LNER No 2548 was to be converted into an 'A3' in October 1945. Renumbered 517 in April 1946 and 48 three months later, the locomotive – which was named after the winner of the 1897 Triple Crown – gained its BR number in June 1948. No 60048 was repainted into BR green in September 1952. It was to receive a double chimney in May 1959 and smoke deflectors in December 1961.
John McCann/Online Transport Archive

Seen departing from Aberdeen on 31 July 1955 is Class A3 No 60097 *Humorist*. At this date the locomotive was fitted with early full height smoke deflectors and left-hand drive along with Kylchap blast pipe and double chimney. No 60097 was the first of the class to be so treated; the remainder of the class were modified between 1958 and 1960. The result of this modification was that the engines had a much softer exhaust; however, this caused problems with smoke drifting across the driver's vision and resulted in the introduction of German-style smoke deflectors. *John McCann/Online Transport Archive*

Although originally designed by Robinson for the Great Central Railway, the final batch of 13 Class A5 4-6-2Ts were to be built by R. & W. Hawthorn Leslie & Co Ltd during 1925 and 1926 for use around the Middlesbrough area. The later locomotives had a slightly modified design, with Gresley-style chimneys and lower domes. This batch of locomotives was allocated Nos 9830-42 under the LNER renumbering scheme and thus became BR Nos 69830-42 under BR. On 22 October 1955 No 69833 is seen at Newcastle Central station with the ECS from a local from Darlington. No 69833 was completed in October 1925 and was destined to be the first of the batch to be withdrawn, succumbing in April 1957. The last of the later locomotives was to be withdrawn in December 1958; ironically a number of the ex-GCR locomotives survived longer, the last not being withdrawn until November 1960.

Tony Wickens/Online Transport Archive

Peppercorn 'A2' No 60533 *Happy Knight* recorded at Doncaster shed on 12 May 1956. Completed at Doncaster Works in April 1948, No 60533 carried its BR number from new and was named after the winner of the 1946 2,000 Guineas at Newmarket. One of the class based in England, No 60533 was allocated to New England shed, Peterborough, for some years, from where it was withdrawn in June 1963; it was one of two of the class that succumbed that year.
Tony Wickens/Online Transport Archive

A record breaker stilled: on 12 May 1956 'A4' No 60022 *Mallard* stands outside the ex-GN shed at Retford having failed on an East Coast service. Renumbered 60022 from 16 September 1949 in BR blue livery, the locomotive is seen here in the Brunswick Green livery that it carried from 4 July 1952 through to withdrawal. Completed as LNER No 4468 at Doncaster (Works No 1870) in March 1938, the locomotive was one of the few of the type to be completed with double Kylchap chimney and blastpipe from new.

The double chimney led to improved draughting and better exhaust flow at higher speeds and the fact that it was so fitted may have been a factor in its selection for the possible record-breaking run. Those of the class with single chimneys were modified with double chimney and blastpipe in the mid- to late 1950s; the savings in fuel that resulted offsetting the actual cost of modification.
Tony Wickens/Online Transport Archive

On the same day, Ian Allan Ltd promoted a special service – the 'Pennine Pullman' – that ran from London Marylebone over the GC main line to Sheffield Victoria behind 'A4' No 60014 *Silver Link*. From Victoria the train travelled over the newly-electrified Woodhead route to just east of Manchester where two Class D11 4-4-0s – Nos 62662 and 62664 – took over for the return working via Todmorden and Barnsley to Rotherwood Sidings where No

60014 was in place to take the train forward to Retford and London King's Cross. The train comprised 10 carriages; eight of which were Pullman stock but one was a Mark 1 first – to replace a defective Pullman – and the last was a Mark 1 third to accommodate over booking. Here No 60014 is pictured at the head of the train at Rotherwood Sidings prior to heading south. *John McCann/Online Transport Archive*

On 24 April 1957 the Ian Allan Locospotters Club operated a special from Paddington to Doncaster, for a trip round the works, over the ex-Great Central London Extension behind Class A4 No 60029 *Woodcock*. Viewed at Nottingham Victoria the locomotive is about to depart northwards through the 1,189yd-long Mansfield Road tunnel. On the return journey, No 60029 failed at Nottingham Victoria with its tender brakes hard on and incapable of being released. Removed from the train, it was replaced by two Class B1 4-6-0s, Nos 61008 *Kudu* and 61272.
John McCann/Online Transport Archive

In 1911 John Robinson, the chief mechanical engineer of the GCR, introduced his Class 9N (LNER Class A5) 4-6-2T primarily for express suburban workings from London Marylebone to Aylesbury and High Wycombe. A total of 31 were built between March 1911 and June 1923 at Gorton Works; one of these was withdrawn in 1942 with the survivors becoming BR Nos 69800-29 at Nationalisation. A further 13 were built by Hawthorn Leslie & Co between September 1925 and March 1926 for service in the north-east; these were constructed to a slightly modified design – by Gresley – that incorporated lower domes and Gresley-style chimneys and the earlier locomotives were subsequently modified to a similar style to bring them within the normal LNER loading gauge. Those still based on Marylebone suburban services were replaced by 'L1' class 2-6-4Ts and transferred to Lincolnshire. In June 1957, No 69825 is seen approaching Sheffield Victoria from the east under the 1,500V dc overhead of the Woodhead scheme. This particular locomotive was to survive in service until November 1959; all of the class was withdrawn by the end of the following year.
John McCann/Online Transport Archive

One of the Class A8 4-6-2Ts – No 69881 – is seen double-heading Class D49/1 4-4-0 No 62731 *Selkirkshire* at Whitby West Cliff station during the RCTS's 'Yorkshire Coast' rail tour of 23 June 1957. In all 45 4-4-4Ts were constructed for the NER at Darlington Works between October 1910 and May 1922. These were designed by Vincent Raven primarily for use on fast passenger services in the Darlington and Newcastle area. Following the trial conversion of one locomotive as a 4-6-2T in 1931 to a design by Gresley, the remainder were modified between 1933 and 1936. No 69881 was constructed at Darlington in July 1922 and was to survive through until June 1958. All were withdrawn by the end of 1960 as diesel railcars gradually took over their duties. *John McCann/Online Transport Archive*

Pictured heading the down 'CTAC Scottish Tours Express' on 20 July 1957, 'A3' No 60094 *Colorado* makes a fine sight as it heads eastbound towards Heaton station. Completed at Doncaster (Works No 1795) as LNER No 2748, No 60094 was named after the winner of the 2,000 Guineas at Newmarket in 1926. A Scottish-based locomotive for much of its career, No 60094 was withdrawn from St Rollox shed in Glasgow in February 1964. The Creative

Tourist Agencies Conference (CTAC) was a consortium of nine travel agents and firms that organised a number of chartered special trains alongside their primary business of overseas rail travel. These had first run in 1933 but were suspended during World War 2 to be resumed in 1945; the last operated in 1968. *Tony Wickens/Online Transport Archive*

Shortly after No 60094 *Colorado* had departed northbound, 'A4' No 60012 *Commonwealth of Australia* headed through Heaton station non-stop with the up 'Elizabethan'. Completed in June 1937 at Doncaster (Works No 1856) as LNER No 4491, No 60012 was a Haymarket, Edinburgh, based locomotive at this date. The 'Elizabethan' had been renamed from the summer only 'Capital Limited' in 1953 in order to mark the coronation of Elizabeth I.

Originally timed to take 6 hours and 45 minutes to cover the journey, the train was speeded up by 15 minutes the following year. Steam operation of the express ceased in September 1961 and the service itself was withdrawn in 1963. No 60012 was to survive for a year longer, being withdrawn from Aberdeen Ferryhill in August 1964.

Tony Wickens/Online Transport Archive

By the end of the 1950s, the life of the Raven/Gresley Class A8 4-6-2TS was coming towards its close. The first had been withdrawn in late 1957 and by the end of 1959 only 21 of the original 45 locomotives remained in service. No 69850, pictured light engine at the east end of Newcastle Central station on 12 July 1958, was one of the last of the type to survive. It and 10 other examples were all withdrawn in June 1960. As NER No 2143 the locomotive was completed at Darlington Works in October 1913 – the first of the type to be built – and was converted from an 'H1' 4-4-4T in December 1933.
Tony Wickens/Online Transport Archive

Pictured at York with an up service on 16 July 1960 is 'A1' No 60127 *William Worsdell*. The Pacific was completed at Doncaster (Works No 2044) in May 1949 and was the first of the class to be painted in BR express blue from new; it was to carry this livery until it was repainted into BR green in March 1952. As with other members of the class, No 60127 was initially unnamed; it was officially named after the North Eastern Railway's CME William Worsdell, who held the position from 1890 to 1910, in a ceremony at Newcastle Central station on 30 October 1950. When recorded

here, No 60127 was allocated to Heaton shed, where it had been based since new, but two years later – in September 1962 – it was reallocated to Tweedmouth shed; this resulted in it final years being spent primarily on services from Newcastle northwards rather than south to King's Cross. A final reallocation saw No 60127 transferred back to Tyneside, but Gateshead shed this time, in October 1964 but its use was limited to acting as a stationary boiler. It was finally withdrawn in June 1965.
Tony Wickens/Online Transport Archive